Yesterday's Tides

Edited by

Heather Killingray

First published in Great Britain in 2002 by
POETRY NOW
Remus House,
Coltsfoot Drive,
Peterborough, PE2 9JX
Telephone (01733) 898101
Fax (01733) 313524

HB ISBN 0 75432 774 4
SB ISBN 0 75432 775 2

FOREWORD

Although we are a nation of poets we are accused of not reading poetry, or buying poetry books. After many years of listening to the incessant gripes of poetry publishers, I can only assume that the books they publish, in general, are books that most people do not want to read.

Poetry should not be obscure, introverted, and as cryptic as a crossword puzzle: it is the poet's duty to reach out and embrace the world.

The world owes the poet nothing and we should not be expected to dig and delve into a rambling discourse searching for some inner meaning.

The reason we write poetry (and almost all of us do) is because we want to communicate: an ideal; an idea; or a specific feeling. Poetry is as essential in communication, as a letter; a radio; a telephone, and the main criterion for selecting the poems in this anthology is very simple: they communicate.

CONTENTS

DEVIL WIND

Cold,
Blasts of arctic wind
Storm up rubbish-strewn streets,
Swirling past dark doorways
And curtained windows.
The satanic devil-wind,
Pounding an unearthly rhythm,
Demands entry into the warmth.
Access denied, he screams his fury,
Then vanishes into the night.

Polly Davies

WONDERS ALL AROUND

The red breast on the robin,
colour of the setting sun,
wings of a soaring eagle,
taking it above the heads of man.
The speed of the running cheetah,
when chasing for its prey,
the patience of the mighty grizzly,
while waiting for salmon to play.

The wonders that the world holds
are in nature for all to see,
the delicate form of the butterfly
listen to the buzzing of the bee.
Do not close your eyes or ears,
the world's wonders are all around,
seek out all these pleasures,
they are waiting to be found.

The turning of the tide,
white sea birds on the shore,
towering giant redwoods
that shelter the forest floor.
The world and nature's wonders
make man's efforts seem so small,
let's not take them for granted,
appreciate them, one and all.

Geoff Hume

MOTHER LOVE

I hear an angel crying
for the joy of a child newly born;
a lovely, gentle human being
to live and love, laugh and mourn
through tears of its own;
I hear an angel singing
for the joy of a child newly grown;
a lovely, gentle human being
risen above worldly troubles
down to human foibles;
I see an angel winging
for the joy of someone's passing;
a lovely, gentle human being
taken at last, deserving of rest
among the best;
Lark, risen like an angel
for the joy of a new dawning;
a lovely, gentle motion on
wings of song at our own
Earth Mother's bidding;
Nature, a treasure to behold
though it bring grief as well as joy;
Mother love, a gentle tale told
at bedtime - like a quilt
to keep us warm

Though we be orphans
in a storm

R N Taber

FISHING

In and out they flash
Silver backs glinting
Suddenly a splash
Toad's eye unwinking.

His skin all lumps and bumps
It looks quite rank
The minnows make a dash
They hide beneath the bank.

The net is full of slime
A ribbon of toad's spawn
One stickleback this time
Oh, what a lovely morn!

Then muddy feet they slip
Splash, landed on his seat
His mother, how she'll flip
His joy is now depleting.

Irene Hinton

THE NATURAL WORLD

The natural world we left behind as soon
as we had fire,
since then we have used home comforts and
these we all desire.

You just have to watch Western man when
he is going camping,
that great long house on wheels, a sink and curtains in a forest,
God's nature he's revamping.

Waterfalls he likes to see, dressed
in his mackintosh,
or, in the sea amongst the shells,
green wellies they go splosh.

Great drums of thunder pound and roll,
lightning lights up the trees,
while man jumps in his sleeping bag
copies the birds and bees.

He has forgotten in the West
how others plough and sow,
to keep us all in lots of food,
while he his lawn does mow.

We are moving too far from the
natural ways of life,
thinking we can mould everything
to suit us, will bring strife.

Jean Paisley

SOMEBODY

Somebody should do something,
Who is somebody?
You, me, we are somebody,
Let's do something.
Recycle,
Cans, plastic, glass.
Read labels,
Choose brands in recycled cans.
Walk, ride a bike,
Take a bus, share a car,
Cut down the pollution,
Help save our world,
Unite.
Let's not leave it too late,
Somebody will say,
Somebody should have done something.

Joan Egan

A HAND TO HOLD

All beauteous things by which we live
by laws of space and time, decay and;
of this faltering substance of human life
the very reason why I clasp them
is because they die.
A handful of memories
long ago at rest
'History is an imperishable quest.'
Silent voices, wordless strains
from ancient voices - faltered veins.
Passion that sprang and thought that started
shall unite us all one day.
'History is never departed.'
With wild notes to beg your pardon
of anything troublesome before.
History is but a garden
in which we sound to war no more.
All these, I clasp, touch and fold,
history is a hand to hold,
high muses that fulfil all ages,
the opening of leaves and pages.

Peter Higgs

RAIN

The clouds are full, pregnancy-heavy
Deep-coloured with rich shades of navy
Full of rain
Writhing in pain
Navy-blue rain clouds, pregnancy-heavy.

Lightning, howls so fierce, so wild
Scares to death the unborn child,
Ruins the birth,
Spoils the earth.
But now, temperatures; refreshingly mild.

Torrential rain falls, as clouds burst asunder
A miraculous birth, to a child of wonder
Labour of love
Gift from above
Thrills all life forms, to a rainbow of wonder.

As grass grows rich, luxuriant and lush
And hopes fly high
Rainbows in the sky
People scarcely recall lightning's threatening flash.

George Saurombe

8

GOLDEN LEAVES

Golden leaves falling down,
The wintry trees
And with them bring the thought
Of days such as these,
Golden sunsets true to all,
The scenery around,
Making and sometimes forsaking
The thoughts of this season,
That completed itself
To be eaten into the very ground,
But there are times when
All may not be seen as nature's
Fairest times of all and is when
And where one can visualise,
The many wonders of a very special time,
That maybe a time when the evening sky
Glows a wintry shade of coldness,
This is when every loving soul
May see the everlasting,
A time to ponder on winter's toll.

C Hush

AUTUMN

Now that autumn is here
Do not sit around in a chair
Visit the countryside for a walk,
Take a friend and you can talk.

The trees now are a beautiful hue,
Now they have lost their colour green
Now in golden colours old and new,
the forests are a sight to be seen.

The birds to the garden come
To fill up their little tums,
So have pleasure and watch them feed
On the scraps and the seed.

Do not forget they feel the cold,
Whether they be young or old,
Autumn is a lovely season,
I guess God made it for a reason.

Jean Bradbury

THE GREATEST MOTHER OF ALL

She sustains flora, fauna, mankind and all,
Paints the vivid colours of the sky in blues and pink
And the orange, burnt umber, yellow ochre of the Fall,
The serene beauty of fresh snow, also the water we drink,
Which has wended its sparkling way down violet mountains,
Past evergreen pines majestically standing to attention.

The colours are so vast I am afraid to blink
Lest I miss a subtle change in Mother Earth's generous reflection,
This wonderful mother with bounty to share.
Man has raped and plundered her wealth
To the loss of the rain forest, felled without care,
Extracting her bowels for oil, not a care for health.

For hundreds of years she has willingly allowed man
To enhance life with medicinal plant's precious gems.
Man's greed will ultimately cause disaster without plan.
Greed for monetary gain I would stop if I can,
For God's tears fall frequently on selfish man.

J Baker

LAND'S END

Of all my favourite places
There is one that is special to me
It's the beautiful coast at Land's End
With its breathtaking view of the sea.

There is a steep and winding pathway
That looks down at the rocks below
Wild flowers cling in small posies
They have so little soil to grow.

Soaring seagulls call to one another
As they hover then dip down to the waves
Heavy seas that pound in the winter
Have left jagged openings like caves.

The wind blows cool on the cliff top
Crashing white surf makes a deafening sound
Spray flies up in a wispy white cloud
To settle on the damped ground.

Too soon my visit is over
But I have memories to take home with me
I know I will come back again
To experience this beautiful scene of the sea.

Pauline Drew

THE BEAUTY OF ALL SEASONS

I walked along the quiet lane early in the spring
The hedges showed some tips of green, birds were on the wing.
Everything so fresh and new this time of year will bring,
All this I saw while walking down the lane in early spring.

I walked along the quiet lane on a warm bright summer's day,
I stopped to watch in field near by, the farmer turning hay
Then saw a lark fly heavenward through the sun's bright golden rays
As I walked along that quiet lane that lovely summer's day.

I walked along that quiet lane as autumn had arrived,
Fallen leaves crunched under foot, but the wayside flowers had died.
The fields now brown with ploughing, each furrow done with pride,
These things I saw, when down quiet lane, for autumn had arrived.

I walked along the quiet lane as winter took its grip
Frozen snow to walk through, must be careful not to slip,
A watery sun just showed her face but the air still had a nip,
As I walked along that quiet lane, chilled by winter's grip.

Dinah Court

SPRING SONNET

When spring emerges from the dormant chill,
With all the beauty of a butterfly
Bursting forth from its cocoon, colours thrill
A world long starved of sunshine in the sky;
Cold and grey so long, suddenly one day
A black branch bursts with blossoms starry white,
Crocus paints the hedgerows, daffodils sway
Upon the breeze, air smells sweet, days grow light,
Hearts grow lighter too, countryside awakes
From winter's sleep, on trees new buds appear
and birdsong greets the morning as it breaks;
Migrant birds return, skies are blue and clear,
Starlit April nights, daisies in the grass,
All the world is bright - spring is here at last!

Ailsa Keen

WANDERLUST

I love to wander in the country
To view Nature in the raw
Some of the scenes I witness
Fill me with such awe.
During the different seasons
There's always beauty to behold
From the young lambs frolicking in the fields
To the sunset of burnished gold.
I love the trees in autumn
The bulbs that grow in spring,
The summer's lovely colours
In winter when snow covers everything.
God organises the seasons
And with his gentle hand
He bestows a beauty everywhere
Across the sea and land.
The sea is like another planet
So vast and full of creatures too
With panoramic splendour
Magnificent to view.
I love to look out of an aeroplane
As far above the clouds we fly
To view the wonderful spectacle
As white fluffy clouds go floating by.
There's so much to see in nature
No matter where you go
So many differing facets
So much to get to know.

Mary Anne Scott

Countryside Memories Of A Tower-Block Tenant

I dream of living in a cottage
with roses around the door
as I sit in a cell
of this giant beehive
surveying with eyes half-shut
with vertigo,
the concrete jungle beneath.

My mind wanders over meadows and hills
and changing landscapes
as each season spills its own palette
to reign over nature for a time.
Colours vibrant, alive, fill my memory
while I die a little more each day
in this drab, grubby greyness.

Gently gurgling brimming brooks
the grace of swans on a lake
the country lane lined with hawthorn
the cattle grazing sleepily
fill scenes of joy long in the past
as I tread littered city pavements,
struggling to breathe polluted air.

I dream of living in a cottage
with roses around the door
but the sun is blocked
by this monstrosity of Babel.
The red of the poppy, the green of fields,
the amber of country sunsets
are lost in soul-less city traffic.

In this cage I remain, trapped,
surrounded by relentless noise
longing for silence, peaceful retreat,
helplessly ensconced in concrete
but unable to take root,
dreaming of living in a cottage
with roses around the door.

Efrosyni Hobbs

THE RIVER

Life is but a river
Wending its way o'er the rocks.
Sometimes it makes us shiver
Or gives us shocks.

It flows into pools of calm
And then the mysterious deep.
The sun there gives us balm
The soothing motion, sleep.

What lies round the next bend, we ask -
Good fortune, bad or nought?
As we go about our daily task
What has the river brought?

Joyously over the pebbles it runs,
The happiest time of all,
And out of this joy surely comes
Something that never will pall.

A Hankey

SHOWING US THE WAY

Feel the warmth of the sunshine,
The breeze blowing through your hair,
A feeling of peace and tranquillity,
A gift from nature to share.

The fields stretching out before us,
Golden corn swaying in the breeze,
Watching the wonders of nature,
Sitting in the shade of the trees.

The creatures that live all around us,
Trying so hard to survive,
Showing us the wonders of living,
Making us glad to be alive.

As the night closes in around us,
And the stars start to shine in the sky,
Thank nature for showing the beauty,
The magic that money can't buy.

Lesley Allen

WINTER BEAUTY

Sunset rays brush the winter sky
Coral bands stretch enfolding clouds
As they float away.
Golden streamers weave and twist across the lingering day
On the dark mountain's peak rests the crimson orb
though almost ready to slip behind - not to stay.
Colours of an artist's dream keep changing
Now silver ribbons fasten round the dispersing clouds
As little peeps of fading blue push through
Trying to make their mark on the high and mighty sky.
Trees cold and stark stand in the stillness
their stiff dark branches ghost-like in the fading light
Yet know on the 'morrow, will be fully dressed in foliage green
Just now - must idle stand.

Hazel Wilson

THE ACORN

From a tiny acorn, a seedling grows
Reaching out for sunlight glows
Its solar warmth that gives it strength
A garden of Eden in width and length
In England's green and pleasant depths.

As the acorn grows into a sapling
Becomes an oak tree, woodpecker tapping
Tall and strong describe the oak
That from the tiny seedling it awoke
Stretching out its branches high
Upwards reaching towards the sky
How it came to be, I know not why?

What is England without shrubs or trees
No bird, nor rest, or perch on thee
In medieval England's past
Surrounded by the forest's grass
Its greenery lush, another acorn is cast.

Rebecca Hart

THE GOLDEN EAGLE

Ferocious!
Hooked beak, death-dealing dreadful talons clenched.
Statuesque,
Proud head erect and golden nape aglow.
Unblinking,
From lofty pinnacle her realm surveyed.
Imperious,
She sits unmoving hour, and hour on hour.
Dynamic,
To awesome height all suddenly she beats,
Then wings unstirring, effortless she soars:
Serenity.

George Newall

CREATIONS

Cascading crystal waterfalls,
Silver-strewn torrents gushing.
The erratic wind carrying the leaf,
Moulding the clouds onrushing,
As the resonating caws hop
On frosty Sunday mornings,
Echoing across the heath
In the misty day dawnings.

Rain patters through the trees,
The summer sun caresses roses,
The honeysuckle scent enticing,
Lingers under our noses,
Whilst horses gallop the lea
And the panting fox lies low,
The farmer cuts the deep, rich earth
'Tis the plough bearing the furrow.

Winter with its fragile flakes
Covers the land with a whitened coat
And swans melt into the scene,
The graceful figures afloat,
Tokens of what nature can offer,
Nature with its unrivalled story,
The crocus arriving in beauty,
The oak reaching grandiose glory!

Andrew Gruberski

AND THE CRICKETS CRICK

Crickets crick in the afternoon heat
Grasses sway in the mild breeze of the afternoon
Be still and listen to the water on its endless journey down the beck
Bugs buzz, competing with eerie screech of buzzard high
Circling above the moor
Black broom pods pop in the heat throwing their seed far from the bush
The chattering of the swallows and house martins sitting on the wire
Telling their new broods the way back to Africa
A black furry caterpillar makes its way along the dusty track whilst
All manner of bugs abseil up and down the tall grasses
Blue harebells bend their blue bonnets in the mild breeze
Knocking away a bee buzzing
Spiders' webs caught in the bronzed barbed wire,
A selection of meals suspended awaiting consumption
And the crickets crick incessantly amongst the grasses and wild flowers
Red hawthorn berries grow fat and ripe amongst the succulent
Blackberries glistening in the heat
Oh for a piece of blackberry and apple pie
And as if on cue a cricket sits on a lichen-covered stone by my knee
Then flies off in the breeze to serenade someone else
The far noise of a tractor with sheep bleating carries on the
Sweet smelling, grass-warmed air
Whilst small tortoiseshell and white butterflies fly in the breeze
And the crickets crick their endless songs and the milking ladies
Of the field wait by the gate to be milked, their udders full,
Their liquid eyes shielded by long eye lashes,
Their grassy breath is carried on the breeze
To sit and be still, we would have missed all this if we had but
Rushed on by.

H J Clark

GOD'S GARDEN

God's garden gives us peace of mind
As we gaze in wonder, when we find
A tiny bud, precious to our sight,
Which after some years has again come to light.
We thought it had died, but with God's heavenly care
It has only been sleeping and shows beauty so fair.
So our world is God's garden and we're the small flowers
Which must blossom with kindness in all of God's bowers,
And bring peace and beauty to a world filled with grief,
That wherever we surface there we'll bring relief
To the terrors of life in so much of the world,
God please let thy goodness to all be unfurled.
Just like in the garden grant us peace in the end,
Through the whole of God's world, let all be one's friend.

Jean C Pease

ENCHANTMENT

I thanked the happy couple who asked me there
To their picturesque garden which they let me share.

The lawn spread before me so smooth and green,
The trees stall and stately looked so serene.
Many different coloured flowers mingle
At the foot of the trees mid the path of shingle.

An artist's brush could not hope to capture
The beauty created by God, man and Mother Nature.

Hand in hand they work all three,
God gave the seed man tends so lovingly
And nature helps it through the season,
Do we really deserve such wondrous gifts?
I cannot help but stop to reason.

I looked back as I walked away
From the friendly people I'd met that day,
At the couple who had kindly given me tea
And was honoured they'd shared
Their beautiful garden with me.

P Harrison

THE SUNSET

A flaming scene of red and gold
Swept upwards through the sky,
The colours from the Artist's brush
Mixed with a wondrous dye.

The sun sinks lower in the west,
Red fades to rosy-pink
And in the dusky eventide
The stars begin to wink.

A harmony of pastel shades
Pink, yellow, blue and grey,
Enhanced by fluffy clouds of white
Tossed by the breeze at play.

But now the wind goes to his rest,
The softening tints all die;
The silver moon, the queen of night,
Climbs up the velvet sky.

The earth in silent splendour lies,
The stars their vigil keep,
But nothing stirs this peaceful night
For all the world's asleep.

Rosemary Marshall

PARADISE M'DEAR (TRELISSICK GARDENS, CORNWALL)

The bluebells are jingling in the hedgerows m'dear,
Sunny primroses smile in the bright silver shafts
Filtering through the new greening spring canopies
And piercing the gloom on the wooded path here.

Sunny primroses smile in the bright silver shafts
Chasing away the deep purple shadows.
See the gorse m'dear and sniff its heavenly perfume
Dizzying our senses in long lingering draughts
Chasing away the deep purple shadows
Of winter still in our grey misted minds.
A prelude to the magnificence of summer blossoms
Staging dells and glades with a kaleidoscope tableaux.

The bluebells are jingling in the hedgerows m'dear,
Sunny primroses smile in the bright silver shafts
A prelude to the magnificence of summer blossoms
And long summer days in our paradise here.

Paddy Jupp

MY RAINBOW

Red the fire of heat and passion,
Orange the embers of warmth and smiles,
Yellow the brightness of our star and souls,
Green controls the natural world.
Blue shows depth of sorrow and seas,
Indigo calms the fevered brow,
Violet matures - the season ends.

All the spectrum from one beam,
Imagine how the heavens gleam.
One white light released from prism-
Colours perfect - synchronism.

Every shade of mood we feel,
Reflects in rainbow hues that heal.
Let your spirit fill with light,
Then all around you will be bright.

Pat Derbyshire

SPREAD GLORIOUS THY VOICE

Spread glorious they voice cross meadows proud,
    Sing loud nature's orchestral tune,
Such rapture fulfil now dream's placid desire,
    portray foresight of a glory divine,
hallowed submission unto heaven the same,
    embraced by honour proud to last.
Chirp sweet doves thine love of God,
    aloft floral elegance blessed the more.

All heaven utter sacred upon drifting winds,
    amid woodland copse which emerald stand,
echo triumphant Eden's melodies now,
    even unto shadows the evening to caress,
marvellous radiance light our night,
    'neath stars cluster - crystal to embrace,
whiter than snow thine creation sheen,
    all honour bestowed unto the deal.

Spread glorious thine voice to echo now,
    cross crystal streams 'neath hills high,
amidst placid breeze accord flow sweet,
    upon creation and 'neath caverns profound,
lament in triumph where salvation flow.

'Neath sunshine's warmth wilt thou bow,
    afore rainbows burnished colours anew,
unto eternity's morn shine thy faith in full.

S Kettlewell

THE LITTLE PONY

My caring friend, in passing
Noticed a small pony in a field
Wasted and ill, neglected.
A gypsy's pony, of no further use,
My friend entered the field,
And found the gypsy,
To ask if she might have the pony on her land
Nurture it and with the vet's help, get it well.
The gypsy agreed and delivered his little pony
To the lovely home I call the 'Magic Place',
Sheep, lambs in season, many budgies in a fine aviary.
Two dogs and two fine horses.
I went to stay there.
Running with the lambs, walking with the sheep
Was the little pony, a shiny, black and white coat,
Happy and healthy in his new magical life.
My caring friend could not part with him,
She purchased him from the gypsy.
Now the little pony is loved and one of her
                                    company of animals and birds.

Madeline Chase Thomas

MY ENGLAND

This is my England where I was born
And I gaze at her hillsides which now look forlorn.
I look at her great trees that are now standing bare
But this is my England which I love and I share.
I see the meadows where cows quietly graze
As I gaze at her hedgerows I stand there amazed.
God created this land, its beauty so fair
As he looked down from heaven, he made it so rare.
Yes, this is my England and yes, I am so proud
It's no wonder that I want to shout it out loud.
God gave us this land so we could all live in peace
No colour, no strife, no hatred or grief.
I look at her castles, her towers and moats
I gaze at the sea, at those big sailing boats.
The beautiful beaches at Cornwall I see
Her rich golden sand washed by the waves of the sea.
We come back to Wales, where Snowden stands high
Her peak seems to reach into God's clear blue sky.
Then there is Pendle, a beautiful place
Where witches were burned, oh what a disgrace!
Then there's the Lake District, its beauty surpasses all other
It's the place I could live, yes, with no bother.
Then there is Scotland, so lush and so green
No wonder they say 'It is fit for a queen.'
Yes, this is my England, the land that I love
Given to us from our Father above.
So let's keep it free from racialism and hate
And live close together as real friends and mates.

May Kay

HAREBELLS

Hedgerows, green and lush
With grasses' verdant fronds,
Seemed glowing 'neath the streaming clouds
Wind blows like willow wands.

Patch of shining blue
Graceful harebells blooming,
So delicate their bright, sweet heads,
Flowers so unassuming.

Bright their azure hue,
Translucent veined each cup,
Beckoning me to stand and gaze
To fill my senses up.

Slender stems swaying
Bid me dreamily stay,
But the sky has darkened over
And I must haste away.

Trees gloom against grey,
Air grows chill, rain spatter
I must hurry home; gone the glow,
Rooks caw, wheel and scatter.

Still, inward-looking
Lingers on in my mind
That patch of clear blue harebells etched,
August's glory defined.

E Balmain

AL FRESCO

Running through a field of hay,
Dressed in just my brand-new hat.
Jumping up to seek direction.
What do you think of that?

Distant pheasants calling.
The birds all start to whistle.
But I drowned out all of their noise,
When I stung my 'nethers' on a thistle.

Trevor Napper

PORTMEIRION

The ride out through clover
And thickset fields,
With white dotted lambs
Spray-dipped
In spring-coloured romance.
Then steaming ahead at Port Madoc
And on to the rough arch and Buddha stones;
All prisoners of fantasy
By shore and boat to 'Les Amis Unis'.
The great escape through imagination
Through chequered boards
Played out by poolside and blue-steeped hills.
Leaning on the trifoil doorway
By parked children sitting on fountains,
Nursery rhyme visuals
For the twenty-first century:
Flower pots and golden totem poles
Serving the 'vision'
Of a Welsh country gentleman
Lost in his own world,
And creating for us all
A lasting taste
Of Eden before the fall.

Peter Corbett

THE GREAT COPPER BEACH
(In the Perse Girls' Garden)

The copper, gold, the yellow and the green
Of your bright leaves, O mighty tree of light;
Of all wild beauty in the springtime seen
They flame the fairest under the blue height.

O great, tall tree, I stand, almost adore,
Beneath your branches as they gently sway,
The soft breeze whispering secretly before
Long summer burns your lightest shades away.

I would adore, but past your glory are
Yet richer gold and gleams of deeper green
Away beyond the world, somewhere so far
To sojourners here such light cannot be seen.

I cannot paint in words your flames and shade,
And, if a painter may, the power Divine
Who made you sovereign of the forest glade
Would guide his hand to make your splendour shine.

I think you are, O lightest leafed beech tree
Put here by God to show this glad spring day,
A hint of beauty that in heaven will be,
Tree touched by wonder from far, far away.

Diana Momber

TREES

All the simple pleasures in life are free,
A startling summer sunset pleases me.
Early dawn chorus starting up the day,
Grey squirrels darting between leaves at play.

It is nature that supplies all of these,
Most of all, I love the stature of trees.
I adore them in various seasons,
Watch them for hours for aesthetic reasons.

Trees, big, small, I really do love them all,
Coniferous trees growing straight and tall.
To see plantations of them is the best,
Each a soldier, stood strong like all the rest.

S Mullinger

SANDSEND - HIGH TIDE

Sand-carpeted beach -
Waves break beyond reach
And I marvel such might could be;
Their white-crowned crest
Echoes thoughts in my breast -
Oh! What is more strong than the sea?

Its thunder I hear
By cliffs shaped and sheer
And answer responds from the caves;
As the billows break
And the ironstones shake -
Say, who can turn back the waves?

My thoughts were close-webbed
Till the waters ebbed
And I watched the tide recede;
Magnificent - yet
Its boundaries are set,
By a greater power decreed.

Serene sky ruled -
My spirits were schooled
As I pondered the mystery -
All nature knows cause,
Submits to God's laws -
More potent His power than the sea.

Barrie Williams

BIRDSONG

A silver pebble
Cast into a dawn-grey pool
A handful more
Scattered
Uneven splash of song
Rings
In the faint stars' silence.
The world trembles
Full chorus falls
Like an avalanche.
In the stillness
The world lightens.

William Wood

THE JOY OF SPRING

Spring is here, the plants begin to grow,
Earth peeps through the cold winter snow,
Sun warms up the, world around awakes,
Soft rain takes the place of frosty white snowflakes,
Hedgehogs around, waking up from hibernation slumber,
Bulb shoots burst through in ever-increasing number,
Birds start once more their dawn refrain,
Rabbits appear among the hedgerows again,
Nights get shorter, longer is the day,
Warmth chases the dreary cold winds away,
Smiles appear on people's faces passing by again,
After being glum through winter's snow and rain,
Thank the Lord for blessings from above;
Showered on us with all his heavenly love,
Without winter's time to take a well-earned rest,
The earth could not produce its very best,
Lambs will start to leap, birds begin to sing,
So let us give thanks to God for the joy of spring.

Stan Gilbert

A WORLD OF WHAT?

What here have we got? What has Mother Nature
Taught, or has she decided against us?
Does nature not beckon, like a wide beacon light
As we view the day, that follows dark night?
Earth has to live by certain guidelines alright
Spring, summer, autumn, winter come to mind
And it all, and with them each new hope I find
As green the grass and blue the sky and the birds
That show through, even the weather defy.
And as on that lawn in the summertime I lie
The sent of roses, fills the air, the sweet peas too
The night-scented stock, I smelled earlier, I declare
Nature's perfumes, how they fill the air and the
Sight of each are so splendid too
Nature's wonders, so miraculous, so often, it but
Seems to me, as God is too, to be true.
(I trust they are not lost entirely on neighbour you)
Trees and flowers, sunshine and showers, the
Creating of a garden, that corner where sweetness
But bowers, and life springs anew, it is there if you
Have a care, here, there, everywhere, for me and you.

M Lightbody

SEA

The great sea! An ever-changing face that
hides a world beneath
Of life and death - in autumn hues of swaying
reed and coral reef.

Shades of rippling light and dormant sounds
invade a conscious sleep
A weightless world of wondrous things
are greetings from the deep.

Below this tempest, lashing a mighty rage
There lies the peace and calm of another world
like a cold and empty stage.

Tom Armitage

MY ANGEL

I caught a glimpse of a butterfly
when my heart seemed so terribly low,
I sat on the seat in the garden sun
and for me she put on a show.

Her delicate wings were moving
as though she was saying 'Hello,'
and her beautiful colours were daunting,
so gentle, dainty and slow.

I sat quite still as she passed me,
then she gently came to a stop,
alighting as soft as a feather -
an angel with wings on the top.

She settled so close I could touch her
as she opened her wings to unfold,
such a beautiful painting of colour
a most wonderful sight to behold.

If only I could have told her
how my heart was so terribly sad,
but she just sat there gently moving her wings,
as if to say 'Life's not that bad.'

For a moment we looked at each other,
it seemed that she knew what was wrong,
then she quietly lifted her beautiful wings,
and like an angel, was gone.

It seemed I'd been sitting in heaven
for that moment my fears passed away,
I came in from the garden and started to sing
and thought 'What a beautiful day!'

Brenda D Volanthen

BIDSTON HILL

Let us take a stroll up to Bidston Hill
A bracing wind your lungs will fill
The smell of pine is strong up there
Where nature's magic fills the air
The windmill stands there at the top
With arms akimbo, still and stopped
The slight metallic noise of chains
Where sails are anchored down
He stands there so majestic-like
Surveys old Birkenhead town.

A splendid view you will see up there
Across the Mersey wide
You can see the docks of Liverpool
Right over the other side
You can see the Liver building
With the birds upon the top
It is not really ever so far to go
Why just a ferry boat hop
The dome on the observatory, it shines in sunlight bright
Reflects the sun that shines on high
Like an eternal light.

The gorse is covered with flowers
So yellow and shining bright
The rocks of ages standing there
Bring children pure delight
The lovers walking hand in hand
With lovelight in their eyes
Enjoy the sights on Bidston Hill
As they just stroll on by.

There is Tam-O-Shanter's animal farm
Why just a walk below, with pigs and sheep and little ducks.
Why not pay a visit, it is such a lovely place
It is grand to see the children laugh
With a smile upon their face.

Eleanor Dunn

DRAGONFLIES

As winter turns to spring
the air still has a frosty sting.
But soon the light will be in the sky
and birds that start again to fly.
Throughout the winter they were found
huddled sheltering close to the ground.
Gradually the sun's rays pierce the blue,
now early flowers poke their heads through.
Snow and ice melt away
filling the rivers day by day.
Water runs over the rocks on into the bay
eventually the tide takes it away.
The season moves on even more,
now the temperature starts to soar.
Insects emerge as they have done before
and warm breezes are seen more and more.
Now things are back as they were,
look on in amazement as dragonflies take to the air.

S Glover

RAIN

Running its race
I watch the rain
Trickling down
My windowpane.

Joining its friends
They form a line
Increasing the chances
Of bettering its time.

Pitter and patter
The hypnotic sound
As it travels the window
On its way to the ground.

Dripping and splashing
Collecting together
How interesting it can be
Watching the weather.

Rushing in streams
They group to a huddle
Wanting to be next
To land in the puddle.

That is where
Their race it does end
Accomplishing dreams
And meeting a friend.

Joanne H Hale

FROM THE DEEP

Long tresses glitter, blue surging waters
Scaly curves surround Neptune's daughters
Resting among rocks, illusive watery creepers
Hands tenderly cradle tiniest creatures.
Dancing waves rumba, breaking foam
Beneath mythical maiden's deep blue home
Beauty swims beside ocean's fishes
Catching clams, preparing pearly dishes,
Wearing jewelled corals, oyster shells
Fine scaly fingers create crystal spells
Hermit crabs gaze moonstruck upon sweetest face
Enchanting fishy maiden hides beneath God's chosen place.
Sea horses touch her soft outstretched hand
Silver-tailed fins swim towards seashore's land.
Diving depths, seeking wonderland's coral lea
Fishy friends adore this sweetheart of the sea.
Sitting stately, craggy rocks hide those gazing eyes
Smiling sweetly, catching seafarers by surprise.

Ann Hathaway

THE SEAL

I think that there is a heaven by
These icebergs and rocky pools,
Lying, waiting for the sun to dry,
Not caring much for nature's rules.

The bounteous ocean seething free
Delivers all my earthly needs,
Sojourning here quite leisurely
I pass the time with dreamy ease.

Sometimes I natter, prank and play,
With the other seals, my friends,
Chattering onward from break of day,
Pausing only when the sun descends.

All together we watch Triton's tide
Go in and out, and out then in,
Until scolded by the sea god's chide,
We wet our hairs, and splashing, swim.

Diving down below, we disappear,
Dicing ever with life and death,
Coming up when the coast is clear,
Resurfacing to catch our breath.

The rivulets criss as meltwaters cross,
Trickling over the wintry plain,
The sun shines on pools and rocks;
And paradise it will remain.

Heys Stuart Wolfenden

WAKING BEAUTY

Butterfly dreamboat
Swans on either side of us
A perfumed fog on the lake.

With care, step ashore
Pulling back branches and leaves
By a tree she rests.

One kiss will bring her back to life
The fluttering of her precious heart
Like white feathers in the wind
The rich enchanting aurora
That radiates her being
The fog that covers this sacred water
All will be alive
When she is loved again.

Eyes open - she smiles
The fog lifts and night is day
Death is turned to life.

Drifting hand in hand
Into the horizon glide
Never to be seen.

Rodger Moir

NATURE'S FORCES

At first the wind arrives, it blows and weaves
Bending the trees and scattering the leaves.
The day becomes night with darkness on high
Coal-black clouds are enveloping the sky.
Large spots of rain start in the early morn
Heralding the arrival of the storm.
It quickly turns into a sheet of rain
Washing the roads and flooding the drains.
The room is lit up as lightning flashes
Followed by thunder in noisy clashes.
It draws nearer and grows even louder
One clap quickly followed by another.
Some people grow afraid, some girls and boys
Hands clasped over ears to block out the noise.
Why do they fear the noise of thunder?
So afraid of the forces of nature.

Terry Daley

Morning Gift

I woke this morn to hear your song,
A melody so sweet.
Around my garden you did throng
With fellow birds to meet.
Your notes so pure, so true and clear,
Like angel harps on high,
Exude such charm, delight and cheer
My heart doth swell and sigh.

No overture of Brahms or Listz
Thy music can compare.
It brings to me contentment, bliss,
A joy so rich, so rare.
You fill my spirit and my mind
With ecstasy divine.
No lovelier sound I'll ever find
Than that, my friends, of thine.

Your throat doth swell to lift your tune -
Perfection to aspire.
As roses bloom in balmy June
You set my soul on fire.
You soar to heights unknown to man,
To reach that heav'nly plane
Where flames of passion you can fan
And then re-light again.

But now the time, my heart doth tell,
For me to soon depart,
Although you cast me in your spell
And capture firm my heart.
Until the morrow, feathered friends
I'll say 'Adieu' to you,
And then again my ear I'll lend
And happiness renew.

Lynne Maddocks

REFLECTED BEAUTY

I love to look at nature,
at all the birds and bees.
A beautiful sunset,
summer flowers, or a tree.
But the most beautiful sight of all,
is when I look at you.

Ken Price

LIFE

A seed springs to life.
Nurtured in the warm soil
It uncurls and stretches upward.
Drops of water kiss the warm earth
As the tiny shoot breaks free.
No longer confined, it embraces the light,
And life's adventures begin.
Nurtured from above and nourished from below,
This shoot with its roots begins to grow.
Smiled on by the sun
Made strong by the wind,
Sustained by the gift of rain.

Seasons come and go
And the little seed becomes a tree,
Smiling and happy in the knowing
That it is a part of the whole,
Connected to all of life.
And children seem to know
As they laugh and climb this tree.
The branches hold them secure and safe.
People lean against the trunk to rest.
While others stop to shelter from the rain
And lovers whisper their secrets
Carving their names upon the bark.

And more seasons come and go
As birds perch upon the branches
Singing sweet tunes and telling tales
As they build their nests on high.
Also busy are those busy-tailed animals
Clamouring up and hanging on.
Such anticipation as they all prepare
For the new births that come with spring.

And our tree, so proud, waits too
As she once again drops her seed
And the cycle all starts again,
With the magic that comes with new life.

Pamela Gillies

TRUST ME

In attitude of supplication, I stood
Motionless with hopeful anticipation,
Gift of seed in my outstretched hand.

From highest branches I was solemnly regarded,
With grave suspicion, with appraising eye.

So still I stood, stood still and held my pose,
Mind willing telepathic messages,
Transmitting overtures of friendliness and peace.

Messages received and seemingly understood,
Body language softening,
As branch by branch, twig by twig,
But still quite wary, still quite tentative,
Descending daintily the staircase steps,
To pause, face to my face, eye to my eye,
Assessing each the other.

Trust established and decision made,
A swift swoop, deft selection,
A delicate dry-claw fingertip sensation,
And blink of bright intelligent black eye,
Then flash of blue, green, black-capped feathers,
And it was gone.

It was indeed but one small hop for bird,
But one giant heart leap for mankind.

For in that moment I had held a trust,
For one split second I had crossed a bridge,
To experience fleet and momentary friendship,
But memory to retain for an eternity.

Barry Jones

THE OWL

When in our countrysides
The brown owl hoots at night
Smutty walls and chimney stacks
All seem put to flight.

That blackness past the windowpane
Might hold anything
Anything wild and natural
That moved the earth towards spring.

Anything plane and simple
Any untrampled wood
Or any broken timbered barn
Where once the cattle stood.

Any dark hill or reedy marsh
Out there when the brown owl calls
Anything but the chimney stacks
Any smutty country walls.

D Sheasby

NATURE'S BOUNTY

Trees of beauty do I see
Upon the horizon before me;
Trees of every shape and size,
Of every shade of green;
Chestnut candles on the bough,
Waving on the breeze;
Apple blossom, hawthorn spears;
Blossoms of every hue
The rainbow colours through.

Beneath the lovely perfumed shade
A carpet of God's perfect flowers grow;
Nestling in the vale below;
Bluebells of the truest blue
Primroses of the softest yellow;
Daisies white and buttercups sunshine gold;
What a joy to behold.

In this beauty is man's delight,
To sit and dream and perhaps take flight
From the toils and woes of earthly fight;
And for a little while at least
To rest in heavenly, perfect peace.

F J Smith

DAWN ON A SUMMER'S DAY

That split second just before the eyelids lift
when all is magical
seems to have spilled over
into this waking dawn.

For the first wonder of the world
is the song of an enchanted bird.
Surely its wings must be golden,
its beak silver,
its feathers studded with diamonds
as he pours fourth his pearls of joy
upon a new-born earth.

And as I draw the curtains aside
I see the first faint tremor of leaves upon the trees
like the ghost of a smile flickering
a greeting to their friend the wind
passing through whispering secrets.

And when I open the door
the air is like the caress of an angel's wing
and it sings with a clear, clean silence.

Can it be Heaven is lifting her veil
for a split second?

Judith Garrett

CATHEDRAL WOOD

I strayed
from the path,
into an envelope
of welcome dark,
sealing me
from August's buzzing cauldron.

The vaulted oaks whispered
in eerie echoes,
of rustling leaves
and bristling ferns
against
my cotton sleeves.

We go a long way back,
the oaks and I,
along the old monks' track,
melting into history -
no traffic or technology,
becoming one
with nature's cathedral.

Jennifer D Wootton

SUNSETS

How beautiful are sunsets
When the sky
Becomes a canvas
For changing murals
When clouds become trees and landscapes,
Before our eyes
Rivers of golden light flow
And vanish into an ice-green sea.
When all the time
The colours glow orange, then red
As the last flare of sun dying slowly
Gives way to blue of ever-advancing night
To bring its stars and dreams
Till dawn.

Margaret B Baguley

SPRING

To awaken one morning to birdsong
You realise spring has arrived.
The dark days of winter are over
And it feels good just being alive.
A watery sun can be seen in the sky
Buds have appeared on the trees.
Snowdrops are seen in the garden
Strong winds have turned into a breeze.

The days have now grown much longer
Though we still get April showers
The sun is quite low in the sky still
But we welcome more daylight hours.
Birds are building nests for their young
A promise of new life they bring.
The seasons all have their enchantment
But one of the nicest is spring

Irene Kenny

THE LUCKY ONES

Cheviot, Hedgehope, Yeavering Bell
The very names seem to cast a spell
On the lucky ones.
Born within sight of those ancient hills
Who know the valleys and sparkling rills
Of the border land.

All their lives they'll hear those hills
Calling above life's thrills and spills
Come home, return.
And when their working lives are o'er
From near or far, from foreign shore
They will come home.
To the border land. The lucky ones.

Meg Gilholm

SUMMER EVENING

The sun is going down
    leaving trails of blazing fire
red and pink across the sky.

Day is fading fast
    handing the heavens to the night
the mystery to unfold.

Dreamily, green fronds sway
    in the slowly flowing river
and weeping willows
    dip their branches in the water.

Stone angels guard
    the ancient churchyard,
township of departed souls.

Church bells ring the hour,
    then all is quiet, all is still.
Shadows deepen, darkness falls.

Then, a golden shimmer
    lights the velvet sky
as the moon appears in all her glory.

Shining, palely glowing
    she lights the dark
and guards the secret of the night.

Brigitta D'Arcy

ME AND THE CLOUDS

I beckon to the clouds
That seemingly lull from on high
Time alone is but theirs
A season of quiet - drifting by
Such a world I must envy
Deep infinity - space
May in humility - peace
I depart this harrowing race.

I beckon to the clouds
Feeling lost chance confused
'Neath a canopy of clouds
How can I ever lose?
Consistent in purpose
Knowing precise whence they came
I beckon to the clouds
They hear me whisper my name.

Irene Gunnion

THE FOREST OF DEAN

Every day when the sun rose,
Stained the treetops car-crash red.
Raven song requiem for the night,
Sparrows praised the day's birth,
Swooping over pine needle forest runaways.
Purple foxglove landing lights,
Swaying them in, on the verdigris breeze.
The woods awoke, dewy.
Stretching like a sleepy cat,
To purr away the morning with grasshopper legs movements,
Smile on the squirrels and caress maternally,
Springtime new rabbits, sunlight dappled.
Ancient woodland, wizened old man,
Old, so old, when I was young.
Older when I am gone.
But you'll be still as green,
Ever verdant, ever new-born,
For my new-borns
And theirs.

M Howard

COMMUNION

Spirits of nature
home is here
with you.
Above me, below me
around me
surround me.
As I surround you
with love
Energise my soul.
Let me know
I am welcome
As I welcome you
into my heart.
Together
here
we are united.

Deborah Hall

CHANGING SEASONS

Autumn unchanged
for centuries.
Peacocks echo deep
in the valley of
imagination, copper
leaves of glittering
silver birch.
First of snowflakes
here once more.
A sign Red Robin
is not far away.

Alan Hattersley

SOUNDS OF AUTUMN

Tread carefully,
Then you will feel
Sounds of autumn
Beneath your feet;
For tinted leaves
Are falling fast
And rustling there
In rainbow heaps.
The ripening seeds
And mellow fruits,
Long, long shadows
Striding on stilts;
The scudding clouds,
Splattering rain;
And gusty winds
Play their refrain.
The longer nights
With shortening days
Reveal to us
Autumn's displays.

H Val Horsfall

HOW MIGHTY

From a little acorn . . . the mighty oak grows,
from the tiny seed . . . the prettiest flower.
The merest trickle of a mountain stream,
turns into rivers of such enormous power.

The smallest germ which is seldom seen,
can cause destruction beyond belief.
On the seabed . . . the remains of marine life,
produced the wondrous Great Barrier Reef.

This is nature at her magnificent best,
a legacy for us all to share.
But some care little for wonderful things,
and hustle through life without care.

How mighty they are with their axes and picks,
reducing our woodlands to mere rubble.
Pollution takes place in all our seas,
coming ashore on each filthy bubble.

Great oaks are falling from where they stood,
whose branches spread to enrich the air.
Going forever are the fresh green fields,
in this land that was once so fair.

Our rivers are brimming with dying fish,
their gills choked with chemical waste.
Wildlife is becoming a distant memory,
disappearing from a land they once graced.

Is it too late to reverse the slide . . .
into an abyss so empty and bleak?
Can we bring nature back to the fore,
let the strong be assisting the weak?

Plant those acorns, watch how they grow,
encourage marine life to kiss our shore.
Then once again we can all be mighty . . .
to live in peace on Earth forever more.

John Topham

A Misty Morning

The short dark days before Christmas
are cloudy and misty and damp,
The morning air is cold and wet,
if going you, you'll need a gamp.
The plants are draped with gossamer
cobwebs bespeckled with dew,
A ray of sunshine picks them out
as they sparkle and gleam every hue.
A beautiful picture, in spite of the cold,
another of God's miracles that He unfolds.

Vera Hankins

CELTIC HEARTBEAT

Fast moving great, grey duster clouds
Harshly polish an already well-scrubbed sky
And sigh.
A slogan streaked delivery van
Reading *Pride of the Clyde*
Throwing up fine spray on the cold, wet motorway.
Curls of sheep dotting soft, damp hillsides
Straying far from greystone farms.
Cows confined in lush, milky pastures
By jig-sawed, drystone dykes.
Pheasants by the roads side stroll
Mists on heather, languid roll
Clouds unfurl, draw shafts of light.
Moon is chased by wind and weather.
Velvety caresses heather.
Skies, like nowhere else can form - slip from grandiose to storm.
And weary kestrels call forlorn
Into the city's orange, sodium night.
Ghostly forms all cast around
On the breathing, steamy ground
Making not the slightest sound.

Marilyn Hodgson

SILENT ORCHESTRA OF LIGHT

Dawn slowly awakes from her siesta,
Stretching to reach the ink blue fringed boundaries,
Where the indigo silk curtain slowly scrolls from sight,
Fading into obscurity for some unknown rendezvous,
Whilst strobes of light peek above the horizon,
As if in some ancient game of hide and seek.

Gradually this impromptu performance,
Merges with the adversary night,
Silent chords echo morning's glory,
In this her pas de deux,
Affaire de coeur,
Au fait de complais.

A ballet is performed in gradual motion,
And soon the sun too is tempted from his secret lair,
By the courtesan waltzing to take centre stage,
Where glorious rays finally burst forth,
Chimes without sound, cascade down from pale blue hazy skies,
Traversing scattered passing white clouds.

Mid morning arrives in all its glory,
The golden orb breaks forth with a silent overture,
Set within the now satin azure sky,
The orchestra reaches a crescendo,
As harmonic sounds pervade the atmosphere,
Heard only by the conductor, the Creator himself.

Silent wind chimes, harps and tinkling bells,
Culminate towards the arrival of dusk,
Accompanied by pink and grey cloud formations,
Like flamingo dancers strutting in their feather gowns,
Soon daylight herself fades into obscurity,
Leaving behind the symphony so silently played.

Only those who seek the tranquillity of the day,
May hear music played from dusk until dawn,
Yet not by chance is this meeting of opposites,
At the Alpha of planet Earth,
An arrangement was made,
And the silent orchestra of light burst forth from the void.

Ann G Wallace

THE LANE

I love to walk this winding lane
That smells anew from summer rain.
Thick hedges rise and wildly run,
To meet above and hide the sun
But here and there will break to show
A wall where fern and ivy grow.
And sometimes if I really try
To make no sound as I pass by
I'll see a wren dart from the wall
Or hear the blackbirds chattering call.

It narrows here and winding still,
To where tall elms stand on the hill,
That have the very best of view,
Where I can sit and watch anew
Bees that rush from flower to flower,
And cows that wait the milking hour.
As I gaze beyond the cows,
Between the elm trees lowest boughs
The blue sea stretches far away
With white sailed yachts upon the bay.

There the town lies by the bay,
A million people come they say
To see the gaily coloured lights
And gaze in awe at all the sights,
Or lay upon the crowded beach
If there's a space in easy reach,
Join the queue for fish and chips
Or candy floss and pleasure trips
All the streets are crowded out
So one can hardly walk about.

But here red poppies gently sway
Here the birds sing every day,
Here there are no thoughts of time
No ambitious heights to climb,
Just peace of mind and joy remain
To walk with me this winding lane.

J Feaviour

THE RIVER

Where blushing moorlands tear strewn cheek
Fills becks and streams neath wooded vale,
Rainbowed rays play hide and seek
All round the forces watery veil.
The turbulent white waters display
Splashing and chasing around the rocks.
Through still pastures with blossoms gay
Where the errant dandelion clocks
Release seeded time across deep pools.
Large brown trout watch flies hovering
And the silver spry gather in schools.
Waters glide by not bothering
Meandering down to the sea,
Past sandy spurs and spits of stone
The dogged drifters no longer ride free
As the tides embrace and welcome home.

H D Hensman

WINTER WOODLAND

Drops of mist
From the fence wire
Hang.
Jewels of glass
Bedeck
Branches of lace.
Sweet songs of the thrush
Trill in the breeze
And the pitter patter
Of wet leaves
Brush
Through the air.

There's a carpet of brown
Beneath my feet.
Soft and moist
To the touch.
And all around
Signs of
New growth.
Just waiting
For spring
To
Appear.

Lyn Sandford

MEADOWS SWEET

I love meadows sweet with flowers
And as I lay here, pass the hours
A gentle breeze caressing my skin
Contentment here I seek to win

Hues of pinks, reds, blues and gold
Scattered amongst green carpet bold
Sweet smelling fragrances, fused by day
From heady flowers on display

Beneath the golden summer sun
My ears pick up, a singing hum
Of honey bees, in nectars tent
Intoxicated, with flowers scent

And as I sit, amongst grasses tall
Before my eyes, my private ball
Theatrical nature at its best
As animals perform, oh such zest!

Now see the swirling waters gleam
From rays of sun, sent on a beam
And onto the weirs edge it flows
Cascading, roars, on stones below

Airborne insects around me drone
While queen wasp hides, upon her throne
And songbirds, upon boughs so high
Sing to me as I wander by

Awakened my senses, meadows sweet
You are my bed, my tranquil seat
Serenity now fills my heart
And peace within, is my new start

Ester Francisca Caruana

SNOW IN THE PARK

The path is lamp-lit that cuts through the park,
Four in the afternoon and night has come,
But snow has fallen and all around shines
With crystalline light that holds back the dark.

Here and there dogs roll over in the snow,
Oblivious to their masters' coaxing calls,
And groups of children snowball fight and play,
As homeward bound all wonder - wild they go.

Shadows have become gold and curious blue,
The whiteness of the scene is silver flecked,
Luminous as if with the light of stars,
All, all is changed and seemingly made new.

Snow has fallen on the park, now it shines
Silvered white and gold and curious blue.

Margaret Hibbert

NO BLANKETS

Coats on the bed
And nits in our head,
Flag sauce on dry bread
And four kids in each bed.
All memories of so long ago,
Our Mom did her best
She was put to the test
Of how to look after us all.
She'd always be there
To love and to care
All memories of so long ago
The days would be long
She was there with a song
Always so cheerful and bright.
If you was afraid of the dark
She'd sing like a lark
And nurse you all through the night
We'd have hand me down clothes
Given by those
Who could always have things bright and new
But we didn't care
For we had our fair share
Of adventures and things we could do.
In the grove we would play
For most of the day
With friends we've not seen through the years
We'd ride on our bikes
And go for long hikes
And share lots of laughter and tears.
The times were quite hard
We'd eat bread and lard
And be grateful we'd something to eat.

Though it would have been nice
To have a thick slice
Of a big juicy piece of meat
Those days have now gone
And time just moves on
But the memories are still in our mind
Though we'll never feel sad
For we know that we had
Our Mom's love, so good, strong and kind.

Eve Hudson

EURO MY SUNSHINE

'Euro my sunshine' - a part world sunshine.
You cheer me up when skies are grey,
But if you link up with George with the W
'A better republic' is what I'd say.

Politically I am extremist.
An anti-multi culturist I'd say.
Bound for entire globalism,
And one worldism all the way.

I did not vote for Blair's new labour,
(I've been a lib dem recently,)
But when Paddy resigned and left us,
I had a very angry day.

Mr Bush squeezed into office.
A pretty close call I would say,
I very nearly stood thumb to nose,
With him that day.

But Tony Blair spoke to his party,
And that most generously, I'd say.
Held up the goal of world republic
And human unity that day.

This is my story, this is my song
Brits have been an empire too bloodily long
So merge us in with the EU and US
And that would be good,
For we folk are all human and not made of wood!

Muchty

HEALTH

Do we all appreciate good health,
I guess we don't but it's untold wealth.
We race about till it goes,
Then bad health begins to show.
In some cases it makes us lame,
Then we wonder who's to blame?

No two people are alike,
Not even if you are 'Yorkshire Tyke.'
Some people love to moan,
Where others won't even groan.

Some no matter the pain always smile,
To medical people it makes it worthwhile.
The worse affliction must be to be blind.
It's up to the healthy to those be kind.

To the healthy, I say take care,
Appreciate it, and look after it while it's there.

Pamela Earl

BLUE

The feelings entangles,
Enwraps,
Traps me inside of me.

I'm sinking.
Down. Down. Down.
Enclosing me,
Soft as silk sharp as thorns.

Slowly I reach up.
Nobody there.
Alone again.
The feeling creeps back.

Wallowing darkness wraps me up,
Keeps me warm,
Shelters me from the outside,
Why?

Desperation clings to me,
Like a baby clinging to its mother.
I can't escape.
Stop. Help. Anyone.

I give up.
Sinking.
Down. Down. Down.
Blue.

Grace Sutcliffe (17)

CLONES

In my arrogance I had myself cloned,
My ultimate goal was to possess a spare part machine,
Millions held the same ideology,
I now live in terror, clones took their revenge,
A world of soulless beings - armaged'don.

Pauline Jackson

WHY

Why did you have to die Daddy?
Why didn't you come home to me?
Wonderful things we could have done
Like going down to the sea.

We could have had a fishing boat
To go and ride the waves
Or we could have gone snorkelling
And explored lots of caves.

Perhaps we'd have played cricket
And could have had such fun
You were getting a little bit fat
Made me laugh to see you run.

Perhaps we'd have taken up flying
Up in the sky so blue
Ordinarily I would have been scared
But I was never scared with you.

Why haven't I got a dad
To take me to school like the others
And is that Dad the reason why
I've got no sisters or brothers.

But I'll try to be what you wanted me to be
To remember and like you, be a man,
I doubt I'll ever be as brave as you
But I'll try and see if I can.

Whatever I grow up to be
I only hope you'll be proud
Whether I get to be someone
Or just one of the crowd.

Marjorie Wagg

THE NATURAL WORLD

The natural world was pure and clean like an innocent flower,
                                        what happened to it?
Has nature we once knew, which is taken by men.
Even our seas are not clean as it's polluted with wasted material,
Which is an expensive place to clean, as money is needed
                                        to make it the way it was.

As man always destroys it, our environment is not a
                                        clean place to live in,
It's controlled by men, like machines and cars,
Everywhere which effects our nature,
Pollution is the major factor, it's not ours to keep as
It's filled with bad air.

The trees help a bit but, there is a lot of pollution for it to survive,
Man thinks they know how.
Our natural world is getting so ugly with lots of waste to remind us.

So why is the natural world, so busy with all things around it?
People in a jam here and there,
Never having time for anyone. The natural world was ours to keep,
And no one should interfere with it.
As busy machines like cars take charge,
And man drive the machines, to suit their needs.

In every place it has not made it, possible for us to live,
The natural world is like a free seed where plants, trees and flowers
Need nurturing in an natural world of ours.
To live in this environment, which has got to big for us to live in.
Men had forgotten nature which was man's best friend.

As men have lost the natural world of nature they once knew,
Like evolution as time and life have made them to live like that,
As nature got lost with it and the natural world is trying,
To find a space before men can get hold of it,
If it is still there.

F Walles

BECAUSE YOU WERE THERE

We ambled forward into the colourful twilight
Alongside a loitering brook.
Correlating shades of mahogany and magenta
Fiery leaves falling at the waters edge.
The cyan sky possessed the moment
Then began to construct a brand new day,
Painting the grass a vivid green -
The fruitful woodland in coppery tones.
A solitary moment that will live for an eternity.

Vicky Stevens

YOU SIMPLY WENT BEFORE ME

(Katherine Jane Herring)

You simply went before me
This I understand
But giving up the ones we love
And letting go their hand

Is something I find hard to do
To cope now that you're gone
I have so many mixed emotions
Which just go on and on

You know how much I worry
It's only cos I care
I never knew it would be so hard
Without you being there.

In my dreams you often walk
I feel your hand in mine
And know that when we meet again
That things will turn out fine.

Till then I know you're waiting safe
There with God on high
This was just an au revoir
And certainly not goodbye . . .

Anne E Roberts

TIME TO TRY

Every day brings something new
Sometimes happy, sometimes blue
There wouldn't be heartache, there wouldn't be pain
We could be friends and love one another
From far and wide, not only parents, sisters and brothers
Sharing our feelings, sharing our world
Wrapping the badness tight in a bundle of twirl
Letting our families grow up in peace
Let us show them, let your love start to release
Wouldn't it be great to have peace all around?
Knowing it would suit most people down to the ground
Let's give it a go, why don't we try?
Too much time has really gone by.

How about it?

Anne Davey

A HEART APART

Please stop your being lonely
As lonely's not allowed,
We understand that loneliness
Still lingers in a crowd
Lonely is a feeling
When there seems little left
But loneliness is hurtful
Ensuring someone is bereft.
One is lonely when a partner
Passes by the way
Brighten up that loneliness
Like on a sunny day.
There is company abounding
But sometimes they are still
Not the answer to the problems
That another life may fill.
Please stop your feeling lonely
As there's life there at the end
As the Lord is up there waiting,
For you to be his friend!

John L Wright

COMPARATIVE NARRATIVE

You bring me smiles.
Like a blackbird song.
Like a cooling breeze.
In a hot June sun.
Like a simple phrase,
Of joyous fun.
Like the kindness,
Of a deed well done.

You bring me sorrow.
Like a frozen frown.
Like a broken body
In a blackened shroud.
Like a stolen lyric
From a thrushes song.
Like the dying rays
From a winter sun.
Like a starving child
With the food now gone.

You bring me laughter.
Like a waterfall.
Like a harvest moon
As the crop is drawn.
Like a stolen kiss.
From a lover's heart.
Like a new found friend
When old friends depart.
Like a welcoming smile
When a new day starts.

You bring me tears.
Like torrents from a broken heart.
Like those final words,
When two people part.
Like a sad song sung
With an angel's harp,
Like two old soldiers
In a war-torn world.
Like a fairy story
Of lying words.

Charles David Jenkins

THE THEORY OF EVERYTHING

I struggle with elusive letters
and toil to tame sneering numbers
as I frantically try to forge
symbols to evolve
a Theory of Everything . . .
even the computer is foiled
and bursts into baffled flames.

But I must continue to struggle
upon my crazy cosmic quest
for we must discover our destiny
and acquire wisdom and understanding
to uncover the secrets of the Universe
hidden in the deep dark
surging seas of space.

Our ignorance appals me
for we do not understand ourselves
planet earth - the sun - the planets -
our galaxy - the microcosm - the macrocosm
and the vibrant expanding universe . . .
but one day we will progress
with enlightened minds
until we reach a singularity
beyond space - beyond time - beyond matter
and enter into infinity.

For the moment I have failed
to find the symbols
that I need to formulate
a theory of all things,
but what remains a cosmic dream
will one day become reality.

Stephen Gyles

BE AWARE OF THE MIND

When you are low,
Your mind goes so slow
How do you control the depression
Doctors, or psychiatric sessions.
You get ill, you feel you want to kill,
But when you lay down at night
The Lord hears your plight
Just believe and give not take
If not for the Lord, then for your sake,
He will understand what you're going through
And then you will know it's really true
Church or not, if you believe
The Lord will give
And you will receive.

Wendy Deaves

TODAY

Today I was told I had cancer,
Quite a short sentence but to the point.
Almost in a second my body was invaded,
The clear water of life was mudded,
Filthy with loathsome creatures
Staring me in the face - waiting.
My faith in God dissolved into thin air,
I had no time for Him, I felt alone.
I searched my memory for the life that had been,
A life full of love and involvement,
It had gone - disappearing into an abyss.
Why me? I asked.
I waited for the initial shock to abate,
The early hours of the morning were the worst.
My body I had always treated like a temple
I never neglected it -
Yet here it was, this viscous lump
Invading my care - worn frame.
It must go, be cut away
Leaving my body whole again.
I must take each step at a time.
Patience . . . so be it.

Mary Fawson

PEACE IN MY MIND

Peace, it's such an intangible thing; it depends on the place or the time.
It can be a time of great reflection, or the friendship between mankind.
It is something for which we all should strive; peace
                              with our neighbour.
Them next door, or other countries, let's moderate our behaviour.
Nobody in this world that should starve, please just stop and think.
Why should nations have to die; just for the sake of a drink?

We should all respect other people's beliefs, and of course their Gods.
It does not matter what they believe; that's no reason to be at odds.
It should not matter your colour of skin, or the clothes you
                              decide to wear.
Each of us is born with nothing at all; tell me,
                    is there not enough to share?
Who is our ruler, who is in charge it does not matter a lot?
He or she must not become too important; it should not matter a jot.
Government should be there to listen, that should be our right.
No need for them to flex their muscles; we are not looking for a fight
Peace is such an intangible thing; it should be our right to claim.
We are all in this life together; whatever we are all much the same.

Ken Mills

TURMOIL

Here I am again, early hours of the morning,
A warm bed left dishevelled,
My heart pounding, head spinning
What can I do?

Pain in my neck, my head 'thumping' with pain.
Why have these things happened?
My heart aches once again,
Fresh thoughts spinning anew within my brain.

'If only' these words pound within my head,
With a spreading tightness across my chest,
Where can I run? Where can I hide?
'My God,' I cry, 'Why?'

Fear like a sickness spreads to my throat,
I cannot take anymore of this stress.
Thoughts whirling around in my brain,
My life in ruins, am I going insane?

All possibilities, questions unanswered,
Racing around within my head.
Should I do this? Should I have done that?
Whom should I trust?

'Dearest Lord, what can I do?' I ask.
All of these things seem to be an impossible task
I want to run, I want to hide,
Everything gone, even my pride.

Where do I turn for help?
Oh, My Lord to you I cry.
I turn to you, please forgive my pride.
My foolish, sinful ways from you I cannot hide.

I have forgotten to be obedient to your word,
Pride in my own self-achievement has occurred.
Forgive me! Please forgive me!
Please Love me still, I, your foolish child.

To you Lord, tonight I want to confess.
Confess my foolish, sinful ways.
Knowing that only with you Lord
Can I find the peace I crave.

I turn to your words Lord,
Peace comes at last.
Whatever the daybreak brings,
These words will last.

'The Lord is righteous in all his ways
and loving toward all he has made.'

Patricia Todd

NURSERY NIGHTMARES

A mother bathes her children then she takes them off to bed
Reciting nursery rhymes along the way,
She hasn't realised these poems fill their minds with dread,
To her - a normal end to every day.

'Are all the children in their beds?' they sing as they ascend,
Quite mindful that it is *'past 8 o'clock.'*
It's just part of their playtime in their world of let's pretend,
But from the door resounds a hefty knock.

The children start to scream afraid Wee Willie Winkie's there,
Their mother holds them close and soothes their fears,
She likes to think she is a mum who shows her babes she cares,
She hugs them both and wipes away their tears.

She tells about the Sandman as they jump into their beds,
A stranger in their bedroom soon will creep,
To sprinkle sparkling dream-dust as they rest their weary heads,
To bring them lots of nice dreams in their sleep.

To choose a bedtime nursery rhyme's quite usual for this pair,
She tucks her daughter in first then her son,
Then settles down between them in the nursery rocking chair,
Chose Goosey,Goosey Gander, that's quite fun.

They lie in bed quite spellbound so that neither one has stirred,
'I took him by the left leg,' Mum declares,
The children listen silently they take in every word,
Continuing, *'and threw him down the stairs.'*

But bedtime prayers, however, nursery rhymes must not forsake,
'And now I lay me down to sleep,' begins,
The last words they are hearing, *'if I die before I wake,*
I pray the Lord my soul to take.' *'Amen.'*

She turns the main light off and lights a candle as night-light,
She leaves behind an eerie, dim-lit gloom,
The shadows cast are flickering and move amidst the night,
Their animation menacing the room.

And so the mother's duties have been lovingly dispensed,
To each she gave a kiss and stroked their hair,
She left them both to drift into a fairyland of bliss,
Or was it land of nursery rhyme nightmares?

Christine Blumer

IT'S NOT YOU

It's been so hard without you
Since you went away
Thinking of you, looking for you
It's like that day after day
Sometimes I often wonder
What I'm going to do
I see you in so many people
But of course it isn't you.
I think I see you here and there
I just want to call your name
I take another look at them
They are like you but not the same.
At times I seem to walk towards you
It's just something that I do
Just when I'd like to say 'Hello'
I look again, but it's not you.

David Whitehouse

PETER

A man of many yearnings
Lonely but not lost in himself
Has a knowledge beyond his means
Yet yearns for more each day, it seems
A need to share to tell to be told
Tries the tried and tested, also the unknown
Has an IQ that reaches the clouds
To ask for help is not too proud
Amusing, serious, a glimmer, nay
Twinkle in his eye
A spade is a spade nowt else can it be
Caring to a fault, to share is to care,
Sez he
He's no rocket scientist, but,
If needs be, could be
Explores the bowels of the earth
Until exhausted, indeed
To find answers, problems he overcomes
Mostly,
At his own speed.

Sandra Witt

RHINOCEROS

Durer's engrave behemoth
Descendant of Triceratops.

He lurches on the dust filled plain
A quivering horn capped mountain range.

A tank with sides of dimpled iron
Impregnable to prides of lions

A fossil from another age
That rumbles down this printed page;

He's Rommel in a leather coat
Binoculars around his throat

He's Goering in an armoured car
He's Churchill with a fat cigar

And yet his fate seems signed and sealed
His horn is his Achilles' heel

And as he charges, turns and breaks
The Chinese measure out his fate

Ingesting powdered rhino horn
To keep their old libidos warm

And turn the Durer back to stone
By picking up a mobile phone.

Richard Bonfield

THE NAIL ABLATION

Here I sit so forlorn, toe's all tender and infirm
Yesterday to say the least was an eventful day.
Nail's removed without nerves or worry
Who's idea was this? 'Mine' Oh no not really.
November is a chilly time of year
Sandal's not really seasonable with gear.
But open toe yes this is mandate
No use complaining, my nurse adamant.
Today I've learnt to dress my toes, well nearly
Soak in salt water, wounds all so unsightly.
Then to bandage, don't move dressing, steady -
Not easy on my own and pushing seventy!
I tell myself this will be worth it
To spend next summer painless and fit.
I won't be outdone whilst varnishing others
These two will glow, a beautiful flesh colour!
Can't wait for my full recovery
From this ablation and horrid surgery.
Never mind in two month's time
I'll walk with ease, sadly miss Auld Lang Syne.
The moral of this poem is - show a little caution
Don't wear shoes I have worn, I know it's very boring
How often I have returned from dances almost lame,
To say in disgust, 'I'll never wear those - shoes again,'
A new leaf I now must turn, it isn't really me,
It's no good I have to listen to good advice bandied
Or spend my life in agony and swathed in that old bandage!

Freda Symonds

THE CHIROPODIST

There I was with my sore feet
The chiropodist said please take a seat
Oh will it hurt, my brain ran riot
But I just sat there nice and quiet.

A swift glance around my toes
Where this will lead to no one knows
Soothing cream was then applied
Now there was no place to hide.

Ah! A little soft corn she has found
And still I sit there without a sound
Out comes the scalpel, I'm not sure about this
But I just sit there, in a feeling of bliss.

Time ticked by but I felt no pain
I glanced outside, it looked like rain
Why had I worried about coming here
She's treating my feet with the utmost of care.

At last she sat back saying 'that wasn't so bad,'
No! It's the most relaxing time I've ever had
A little more cream and a dressing in place
Now at last there was a smile on my face.

Christine J Gardiner

PUBLISH AND BE DAMNED

I wrote a book of verse a while ago
A crafted work - it seemed to take an age.
Reflecting back - 'You stupid so and so
Twas doggerel you put upon the page!'

Some foolish dream of taking centre stage,
An ego trip! Of mortal man a curse!
Such vanity, whatever could assuage
The driving force? Things went from bad to worse.

A book evolved called 'Making Matters Verse'
One copy sold, or maybe even two!
No jackpot here; no great prize winning purse,
But still, I made the ninety nine 'Who's who.'

The door's still slightly open, not quite slammed
Strong impulses poetic . . . I'll be damned!

Les D Pearce

FROM MAZDA TO FORD

Part 1.

Dear Mazda, I'm in trouble, it's a cause of much distress
My little car's a Mazda but quite frankly it's a mess!

It doesn't like wet weather and the engine fails to start
If it's rainy or it's snowy and it really breaks my heart.

The windows need replacing to keep me out of harm,
For the rain comes in so wetly and it really soaks my arm.

When it goes, it is an angel and it's speedy when in top
But the brake pipe, it is leaking and I fear the car won't stop!

The tyres aren't so clever, though I pump them up each week
And the bodywork needs derusting, it's a miracle that I seek.

I work in the community with the patients in the town
For those people's needs, it's crucial, and I must not let them down.

I have to have a car for work and I don't want you to be harassed
But when I go out in my rust heap, I really feel embarrassed.

I don't like to be a bother, it really makes me squirm
But I can't afford a new car and I don't know where to turn.

So if you like a challenge or you want to show you care
Please say you'll do my car up and make me a happy Clare.

they didn't so . . .

Part 2.

Alas and alack, why did you write back to tell me you couldn't assist,
My engine's all broke, tho' I pull out the choke all I get
is a fine spray of mist.

The body's all worn, all tatty and torn, one day it will suddenly bust.
It's not in my head, the spots are quite red, it has third
degree patches of rust!

It's a very old car and it's gone very far and I know that
                                        I'm not being fair
It looks at me sadly as if I'm treating it badly but deep
                                down I really do care.

It won't pass its MOT cos the big ends are shot and I can't
                                drive the old thing abroad,
The paintwork is flaking, my poor car is breaking
                                the bank which I just can't afford.

The prognosis is poor and I'm not very sure of the home
                                        that my poor car came from.
The door's got a dent, the bumpers are bent and yet it still
                                        goes like a bomb!

The carpets are soggy, the demister's foggy, the heater
                                won't work anymore.
I lay lots of tin where the water comes in cos there's
                                ruddy great holes in the floor.

The oil consumption is too high to mention
                                and I know that you must be dismayed.
I'll write any old hash as I ain't got the cash cos
                                us nurses are so poorly paid.

Please don't write again, for I can't stand the pain and
I'm sure that you must be quite bored,
The end of an era is getting much nearer,
Perhaps I'll just buy me a Ford!

Clare Caldicott

WHAT HAS SHE DONE TO ME?

I sometimes sit and wonder
What has she done to me?
I sit alone in our home
Missing her company
I never thought the future
Would be without my wife
Will I ever regain happiness?
And lead a normal life.

Whilst she became deceitful
My love for her flowed free
Now I sometimes sit and wonder
Did you plan to ruin me?
This life she tried destroying
Will never be the same
Anger, pain and torment
Can I ever love again?

I'm trying yes I'm trying
To overcome these awful days
But my mind keeps recalling
Her evil, adulterous ways
I know she's not returning
No reunion can there be
So I sometimes sit and wonder
What has she done to me?

Jason Davies

TEAR OF SADNESS

A tear once more
In your eye
Tear of sadness
Not of joy
Unanswered questions
We understand why
That lonely tear
Drops from your eye.

A saddened heart
Saddened life
All because
Of an adulterous wife
Explanations
She didn't say
Just packed her case
And went away.

As life rebuilds
For you again
Without the torment
Anger and pain
That saddened tear
You'll always cry
Just like your love
It will not die.

Dennis Davies

TIME TO GET FIT

I knew a fat old lady -
Who wobbled when she walked,
Her teeth - they didn't fit her
And rattled when she talked.

'You must go to your dentist,'
Her neighbour kindly said,
For the lady was discontented -
And confined herself to bed.

Then one day the neighbour said -
'We're going to the gym,'
'Oh no!' she said, 'I'm much too old,
To think of getting thin.'

''Nonsense' when you get there -
You'll find it does you good,
Instead of sitting in a chair -
Scoffing chocolate pud.'

'Alright' she said and wandered out,
In weeks she'd lost some weight,
Her teeth - they didn't move about
And she gave up eating cake.

Wendy Watkin

DEMENTED

'Demented' how would I be able to pay,
Different 'Bills,' were arriving every day.
Reminding me, the amount, I must pay.
I tried to relax, unable to sleep,
When on the telephone, I heard 'Chris Tarrant' say,
You are invited, to come here and play,
'Who wants to be a millionaire,' today.
I cleaned my shoes, pressed my suit,
I may be poor, but tidy I would look.
I dreamt I was walking on air,
When the train, and the taxi took me there.
I answered the test question like a flash,
While on the rostrum, many questions, Chris Tarrant asked,
My answer's were coming from out of the blue,
I was surprised, each of my answers was true.
Whilst in a trance, I heard Chris say,
'A millionaire, you are today.'
From rostrum I began to walk,
That is when, I heard my dog bark,
I really was walking on air,
I awoke at the foot of the stairs,
My dream of a fortune, quickly faded away,
A broken leg, I was rewarded with today . . .

Brian Marshall

SNORING

If you're in trouble just like me,
Your in your house what can it be.
There's this awful huffing and puffing noise, just like a pig.
It must be something terribly big.

I'm in my bed and trying to sleep quite quiet,
It sounds like someone's starting a riot.
Then I begin to realise just what it is,
It's just my partner doing the biz.

He's snoring as you may have guessed,
I just wish that he'd have a rest.
After while he quietens down,
All I can do is turn round and frown.

By now I'm very worn out and disturbed,
And he sleeps on and hasn't heard.
I may just get a wink of sleep or so,
As he may not realise and never know.

I expect I'll go through it again tomorrow night,
Then I will be in the same plight.
I took him on for better or worse,
But really love him although he is a curse.

Eileen Denham

SAFETY FIRST

Scientists work on projects
which does not help the nation
it seems they are only interested in
this human cloning operation.

With the flooding and the deaths around
they should be worried here
as this has become a common thing
which has brought many people fear.

It is put down to global warming
according to many institutions
so the scientists should be working here
to find out the true solution.

They are more concerned in creating babies
through test-tube experiments
than tackling the destruction by the floods
which is causing discontent.

We are finding bother with our food
in breeding animals for our meat
as some is found contaminated
and most unfit to eat.

Lachlan Taylor

THE RIVER

As I flow towards the sea,
not many people stand still
and stare, or think about me,
until I reach the foaming sea.

I start from a hidden spring
in the hills, far away.
Flowing through the fields,
to reach the salty sea.

I pass by the town and homes,
by palaces and Bishops see,
not stopping for anything,
until I reach the open sea.

Trees grow along my banks,
creatures hide in a branch.
Children bathe in water clear,
I go on to the sea.

When at last the sea I reach,
I see children on the beach,
playing in sand and sea.
Still no thought for me.

The ocean roars me on,
I am lost in its foam.
Here, for ever I will be
lost in the restless sea.

John Harrold

DAWN - OUTSIDE THE WINDOW

I looked out of the window, it was just gone five o'clock,
I don't quite know what woke me up, probably an itchy leg,
The dawn crept down the garden, past the bushes and the shed,
I would have missed this magic scene if I had stayed in bed.

The garden looked all peaceful, as I looked out again,
Then all at once, it started bloody peeing down with rain,
That made me feel all chilly, so I shot back into bed,
Before I'd gone to bed last night, the sky was streaked with red!

If this delighted shepherds, they must all be bleedin' thick,
Cos I take no delight in rain, it gets right on my wick,
It spoilt that magic morning scene that touched my poets' heart,
Seeing dawn creep down the garden gave my day a wondrous start.

Mick Nash